EDGE
BOOKS™

BLOODIEST BATTLES

IMPOSSIBLE VICTORY

THE BATTLE OF STALINGRAD

BY ERIC FEIN

CONSULTANT:
Roger Reese, PhD
Professor of History
Texas A & M University

Capstone
press®
Mankato, Minnesota

Edge Books are published by Capstone Press,
151 Good Counsel Drive, P.O. Box 669, Mankato, Minnesota 56002.
www.capstonepress.com

Library of Congress Cataloging-in-Publication Data
Fein, Eric.
    Impossible victory: the Battle of Stalingrad / by Eric Fein.
    p. cm. — (Edge books. Bloodiest battles)
    Includes bibliographical references and index.
    Summary: "Describes events before, during, and after the Battle
of Stalingrad, including key players, weapons, and battle tactics" — Provided
by publisher.
    ISBN-13: 978-1-4296-1937-0 (hardcover)
    ISBN-10: 1-4296-1937-6 (hardcover)
    1. Stalingrad, Battle of, Volgograd, Russia, 1942–1943 — Juvenile literature.
I. Title. II. Series.
D764.3.S7F44 2008
940.54'21747 — dc22   2008002002

Editorial Credits

Kathryn Clay, editor; Bob Lentz, designer/illustrator; Jo Miller,
    photo researcher

Photo Credits

Alamy/Mary Evans Picture Library, 12, 29
AP Images, 10, 13 (top), 18–19
Getty Images Inc./Hulton Archive, 15; Keystone, 7, 13 (bottom); Slava
    Katamidze Collection/Georgi Zelma, 4; G.Lipskerov, 24
The Granger Collection, New York, 16; ullstein bild, 14, 23, 26
The Image Works/LAPI/Roger-Viollet, cover (bottom); Mary Evans/Meledin
    Collection, cover (top); Topham, cover (middle)
Zuma Press/Keystone Pictures Agency, 6

1 2 3 4 5 6 13 12 11 10 09 08

TABLE OF CONTENTS

CHAPTER 1

REASONS TO FIGHT

After the Germans bombed Stalingrad on August 23, 1942, Soviet soldiers fought in the rubble of their former city.

During World War II (1939–1945), hundreds of battles took place. None of these battles were as deadly as the Battle of Stalingrad. From August 1942 to February 1943, Germany fought against the Soviet Union to control the city of Stalingrad.

Over the course of the battle, more than 1 million people were killed, and the city was destroyed. The Soviets were finally able to beat the Germans. But in a battle this bloody, both sides suffered great losses.

FACT:

> NON-AGGRESSION PACT

In August 1939, Germany and the Soviet Union signed a non-aggression pact. This meant the two countries would not attack each other. The Germans broke this agreement when they invaded the Soviet Union in June 1941.

Nazi Germany

In Germany, the **Nazi Party** controlled the government. Adolf Hitler led the party. He became the **chancellor** of Germany on January 30, 1933.

After its defeat in World War I (1914–1918), Germany was forced to pay for damages it caused during the war. As a result, Germany suffered many economic and social troubles. The Nazis promised to fix these problems. However, Hitler planned to do more than just solve Germany's problems. He wanted to conquer the world.

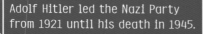

Adolf Hitler led the Nazi Party from 1921 until his death in 1945.

Communist Russia

The Communist Party took control of Russia after winning the Russian Revolution of 1917. In 1922, the party formed the Soviet Union, or the U.S.S.R. Joseph Stalin became the leader of the U.S.S.R. in 1929.

Nazi Party – a group led by Adolf Hitler that ruled Germany from 1933 to 1945

chancellor – a title for the leader of a country

Operation Barbarossa

In June 1941, Hitler launched his invasion of the Soviet Union. This invasion was code-named Operation Barbarossa. The goal was to capture the cities of Moscow and Leningrad, as well as Soviet oil fields. Moscow was the Soviet Union's capital city.

Why Stalingrad?

By late 1941, Hitler's plans to capture Leningrad and Moscow had failed. He then decided to attack Stalingrad. He did this for several reasons. First, it was an important industrial city. Factories there made the Soviet T-34 tanks, and Hitler wanted to stop tank production. Second, Stalingrad was located along the Volga River. This made it easy to transport tanks and supplies to other parts of the Soviet Union. Third, the city was close to oil fields. The Soviet oil supply would help fuel German tanks. Finally, Hitler wanted to capture the city for what its name represented. Stalingrad was named after Soviet leader Joseph Stalin. Hitler hoped that taking Stalin's city would crush the Soviets' spirit.

NORWAY

DENMARK

GREATER GERMANY

ITALY

CROA

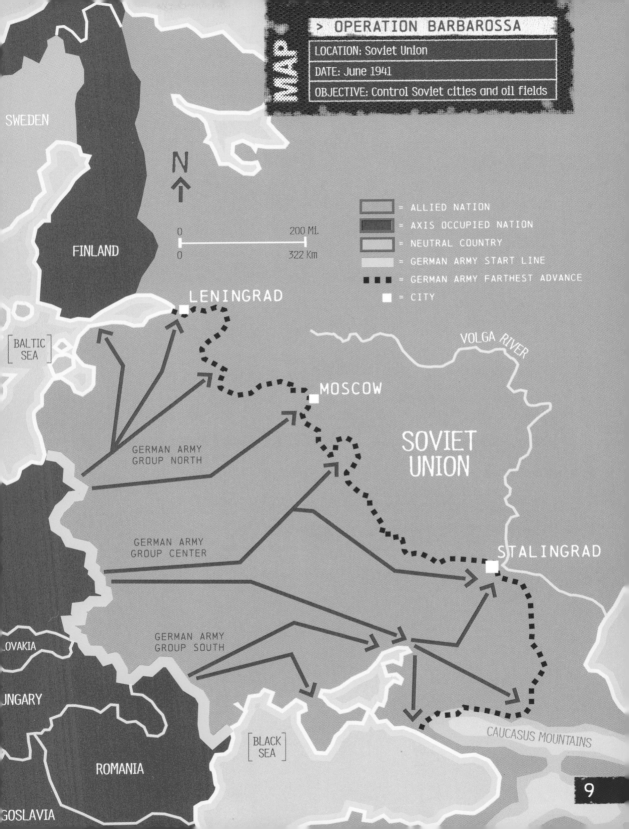

SWEDEN

FINLAND

> OPERATION BARBAROSSA

LOCATION: Soviet Union

DATE: June 1941

OBJECTIVE: Control Soviet cities and oil fields

N

0   200 Mi.
0   322 Km

☐ = ALLIED NATION
■ = AXIS OCCUPIED NATION
☐ = NEUTRAL COUNTRY
▬ = GERMAN ARMY START LINE
▪▪▪ = GERMAN ARMY FARTHEST ADVANCE
☐ = CITY

LENINGRAD

[BALTIC SEA]

VOLGA RIVER

MOSCOW

SOVIET UNION

GERMAN ARMY GROUP NORTH

GERMAN ARMY GROUP CENTER

STALINGRAD

GERMAN ARMY GROUP SOUTH

OVAKIA

JNGARY

[BLACK SEA]

CAUCASUS MOUNTAINS

ROMANIA

GOSLAVIA

9

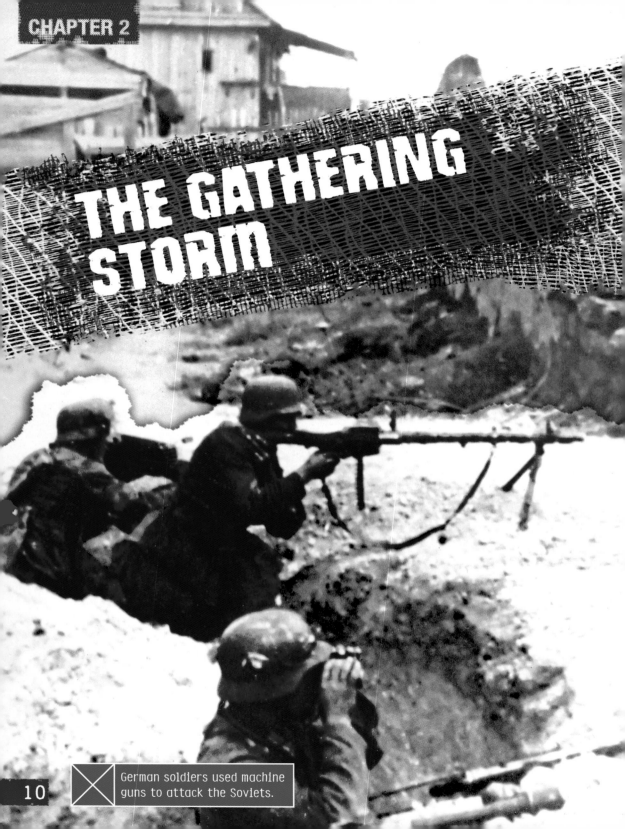

CHAPTER 2

THE GATHERING STORM

German soldiers used machine guns to attack the Soviets.

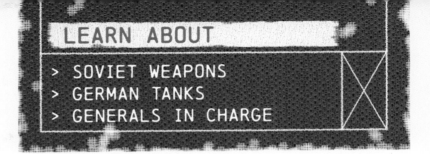
In the months before the Battle of Stalingrad, the German Army had more than 6 million soldiers in Russia. They also had more than 3,000 tanks and 3,400 aircraft.

The Germans captured about 2.5 million Soviets and killed nearly 5 million more. Despite the heavy losses, the Soviets refused to give up. Some German commanders were concerned about how tough the Soviets were. The Germans were right to be worried.

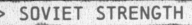

FACT:

> SOVIET STRENGTH

German writer Edwin Dwinger wrote about injured Soviet soldiers who had been taken prisoner. Some had been badly burned by German flamethrowers. One soldier had his jaw shot off. None of the prisoners cried out or moaned in pain.

Soviet Might

When Germany first invaded the Soviet Union, Soviet weapons were not as good as Germany's. However, Stalin put pressure on the workers in the weapons factories to make better weapons faster. One such weapon was the T-34 tank. In 1942, the T-34 was considered better than any of the tanks Germany was using.

The Soviets also had Katyusha rocket launchers and Ilyushin IL-2 planes. The Katyusha could launch many rockets at the same time. The Ilyushin IL-2 was easy to fly and hard to destroy.

Katyushas were often attached to trucks, so they were easy to move.

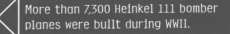
More than 7,300 Heinkel 111 bomber planes were built during WWII.

The German War Machine

The German air force was called the Luftwaffe. They planned to use the JU-88, the Heinkel 111, and the Stuka dive-bomber planes to attack Stalingrad.

The German tanks, called Panzers, were another important part of the German attack plans. Each tank was armed with a cannon and two machine guns.

Panzers could reach a top speed of 40 miles (64 km) per hour.

General Paulus served in the German Army for 32 years before leading the Sixth Army.

Men of War

Hitler put General Friedrich Paulus and the Sixth Army in charge of capturing Stalingrad. Hitler assigned the Fourth Panzer Army to assist Paulus. Because they were **allies**, troops from Romania, Italy, and Hungary also helped the Germans.

allies — people, groups, or countries that work together for a common cause

Soviet General Georgy Zhukov was in charge of protecting the Stalingrad front. Zhukov had previously stopped the Germans from capturing Leningrad. The responsibility of protecting the city went to General Vasilii Chuikov and his Sixty-Second Army.

The Germans were about to launch one of the bloodiest battles in history. The Soviets stood ready to defend their city.

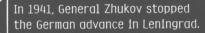

In 1941, General Zhukov stopped the German advance in Leningrad.

CHAPTER 3

THE BATTLE BEGINS

German dive-bombers destroyed Soviet railroads, roadways, and aircraft.

On August 23, 1942, German dive-bombers filled the sky above Stalingrad. The citizens ran for cover, but there was no place to hide. Within minutes of the Luftwaffe's air assault, most of Stalingrad was burning.

The Luftwaffe flew more than 600 planes over the city the first day. These planes dropped more than 1,000 tons of bombs over Stalingrad. The bombings destroyed the city. More than 40,000 Soviet **civilians** and soldiers were killed. Buildings, homes, and schools were burnt to the ground. Roadways were ruined. After the bombing raid, the German soldiers surrounded the city.

civilian — a person who is not in the military

War of the Rats

The Soviets kept the Germans outside Stalingrad for several weeks. But on September 13, German troops managed to invade the city. They tried to reach Chuikov's command post but had few places to take cover. Chuikov stationed snipers to shoot unprotected German soldiers.

Bombing Stalingrad had been a mistake. The streets were full of rubble, and German tanks could not move easily through the streets. This forced the Germans to change their plans. Without their tanks, soldiers fought in sewers and bombed-out buildings. The Germans called this kind of combat *Rattenkrieg*, or "rat's war."

The Soviets Strike Back

On November 19, 1942, German soldiers relaxed in their camp 100 miles (161 kilometers) west of Stalingrad. This calm was shattered at 7:20 in the morning when Soviet T-34 tanks roared into view. The Soviets had launched a daring attack that would surround the Germans. They named the attack Operation Uranus. The Soviets attacked the Germans with ammunition from 3,500 cannons. The cannons were heard up to 8 miles (13 kilometers) away.

In Stalingrad, a similar attack had begun. Before the day's end, Soviet soldiers had killed or captured more than 75,000 German and Romanian soldiers. The strikes continued for four days. Then the two Soviet forces met up west of Stalingrad and surrounded their enemies. The Germans were trapped.

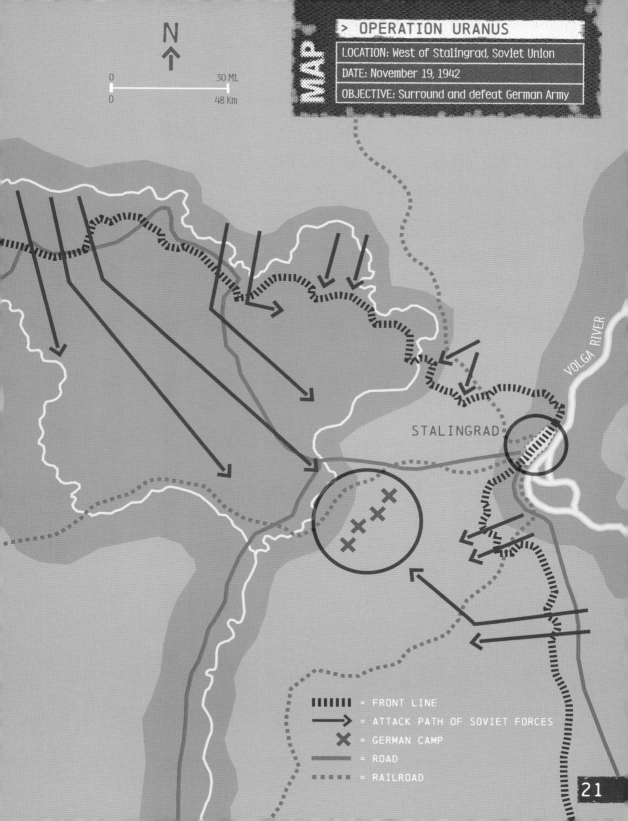

N

| 0 | | 30 ML |
| 0 | | 48 Km |

VOLGA RIVER

STALINGRAD

IIIIIII = FRONT LINE
———▶ = ATTACK PATH OF SOVIET FORCES
✕ = GERMAN CAMP
——— = ROAD
••••• = RAILROAD

Saving the Sixth Army

German officers begged to join up with the rest of the German army, but Hitler refused. Instead, Hitler created a special army to rescue the Sixth Army. He put Field Marshal Erich Von Manstein in command. But a December blizzard and a strong Soviet defensive stopped Von Manstein's troops 30 miles (48 kilometers) from Stalingrad.

> NUREMBERG TRIALS

At the end of World War II, many German military officials were arrested for committing war crimes. Their trials took place from 1945-1949 in Nuremberg, Germany.

In 1949, Field Marshal Von Manstein was convicted of failing to protect civilians during World War II. He was sentenced to 18 years in prison. The sentence was later reduced to 12 years. He was released for medical reasons in 1953 after serving only four years.

Just before surrendering, General Paulus
was promoted to Field Marshal.

The Hopeless Winter

The Germans had expected a quick victory. They weren't prepared for the harsh Soviet winter. Troops ran out of medical supplies and food. Soldiers had to kill their horses for food. Once all the horses were eaten, the Germans ate rats. Many German soldiers tried to escape these brutal conditions. Soldiers caught trying to escape were often shot by fellow German soldiers. Some soldiers killed themselves.

Meanwhile, Soviet forces tightened around the Germans. German planes could no longer take off or land. Wounded soldiers could not be flown to safety. Still, Hitler urged his troops to fight to the death. By December, the German soldiers were dying from lack of food. Many were so weak they could not lift their weapons.

The Germans fought as best they could. But they were no match for the better-equipped Soviet forces. To save the lives of his remaining men, Paulus asked for permission to surrender. Hitler refused. Without Hitler's permission, Paulus surrendered to the Soviets on January 31, 1943. The final members of his Sixth Army surrendered on February 2, 1943. The battle was over.

CHAPTER 4

A GREAT LOSS

After the battle, the once busy streets of Stalingrad were quiet and filled with rubble.

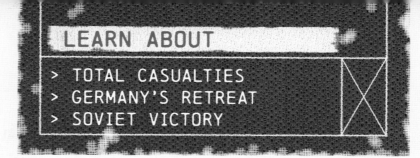
The Battle of Stalingrad was one of the bloodiest battles ever fought. Of the 250,000 German soldiers sent to Stalingrad, fewer than 91,000 survived. These survivors were taken to prisoner of war camps. Many were overworked or starved to death after the war. Only about 5,000 German soldiers ever made it back to Germany.

The Soviet losses were massive. About 1.1 million Soviet civilians and soldiers were wounded or killed. Stalingrad's population was nearly half a million people before the battle. Afterward, only about 1,500 Stalingrad citizens remained in the city. The rest had escaped before the invasion or were killed during the fighting.

Stalingrad was now a huge graveyard. The streets were filled with the bodies of soldiers. The burnt remains of tanks and other vehicles littered the ground. Factories, homes, and schools were crushed.

German Failure

The Germans lost the battle because Hitler refused to listen to his commanders. He made decisions based on feelings and not sound military advice. Hitler attempted to capture the oil fields and take Stalingrad at the same time. When his officers advised against this, Hitler ignored them.

The Final Result

The defeat at the Battle of Stalingrad ended Germany's invasion of the Soviet Union. After losing almost an entire army, the Germans were forced to retreat. Germany never fully recovered from the loss.

The victory at Stalingrad made the Soviet military more confident. With this confidence, the Soviet Union became a superpower. The country's influence over world events lasted nearly 50 years.

After their victory, Soviet soldiers celebrated with their families.

allies (a-LYZ) — people, groups, or countries that work together for a common cause

chancellor (CHAN-suh-luhr) — a title for the leader of a country

civilian (si-VIL-yuhn) — a person who is not in the military

communist (KAHM-yuh-nist) — relating to communism; communism is a way of organizing a country so the land, houses, and businesses are operated by the government.

flamethrower (FLAYM-throw-uhr) — a weapon that shoots a stream of burning liquid

industrial (in-DUHSS-tree-uhl) — having to do with businesses and factories

Katyusha (ka-tee-USH-a) — a Soviet rocket launcher of World War II

Nazi Party (NOT-see PAR-tee) — a political party led by Adolf Hitler; the Nazis ruled Germany from 1933 to 1945.

Panzer (PAN-zur) — a German tank of World War II

sniper (SNY-pur) — a soldier trained to shoot at long-distance targets from a hidden place

READ MORE

Adams, Simon. *World War II.* DK Eyewitness Books. New York: DK, 2004.

Boyd, Bentley. *World War 2 Tales.* Williamsburg, Va.: Chester Comix, 2005.

Williams, Brian. *Life As a Combat Soldier.* World at War — World War II. Chicago: Heinemann, 2006.

INTERNET SITES

FactHound offers a safe, fun way to find Internet sites related to this book. All of the sites on FactHound have been researched by our staff.

Here's how:
1. Visit *www.facthound.com*
2. Choose your grade level.
3. Type in this book ID **1429619376** for age-appropriate sites. You may also browse subjects by clicking on letters, or by clicking on pictures and words.
4. Click on the **Fetch It** button.

FactHound will fetch the best sites for you!

INDEX